DRAMA *for* WORSHIP

Volume 1

DRAMA *for* WORSHIP

Contemporary Sketches
for Opening Hearts to God

Curt Cloninger

Standard Publishing
Cincinnati, Ohio

Drama for Worship, Volume 1
© 1999 by Curt Cloninger
All rights reserved

The Standard Publishing Company, Cincinnati, Ohio
A division of Standex International Corporation
Printed in the United States of America

Designed by Steve Diggs and Friends
Edited by Lise Caldwell

06 05 04 03 02 01 00 99   5 4 3 2 1

Library of Congress Cataloging-in-Publication Data

Cloninger, Curt.
    Drama for worship / Curt Cloninger.
        p. cm.
    Contents: v. 1. 8 sketches and monologues — v. 2. 8 sketches and monologues.
    ISBN 0-7847-0916-5
    1. Drama in public worship.   2. Christian drama, American.
    I. Title.
BV289.C57   1999   98-44071
246'.72—dc21

For Tish and Kap and Lily

Contents

How to Use This Hammer

They should come with warning labels; hammers, saws and the like. "Caution: In the right hands, this hammer will prove extremely effective for many household projects. In the wrong hands, someone could lose a thumb." Some folks are great with household implements. Not me. More than once, I've come close to losing a thumb. But, I've got this friend, Mark, who's a whiz with tools. So, usually, when I'm faced with a major household project, I give Mark a call and he comes right over, tools in hand. He swiftly (and painlessly) cuts the needed trim work or patches the gaping Sheetrock hole. I stand and watch in amazement. When Mark's done, I thank him profusely and he mumbles a reply. Something like, "Aww, it's nothing. You just gotta have the right tools and know how to use 'em." Exactly. That's why I give Mark a call in the first place. He's got the right tools and he knows how to use 'em.

So, you're doing theater in your church. You're maybe in the "banging your thumb" stage, or maybe you're already doing some incredible handiwork. But, there's one thing for sure; whether you're just getting started with church drama, or whether you're a seasoned theater veteran, it always helps to have the right tools. I've learned that one of the foundational tools in any theater situation is a good script. Hopefully, this book will provide you with that tool.

This book is full of what I like to call "Good Used Scripts." These scripts have been around the block a time or two. They've been tested, critiqued, and picked over, by actors in the rehearsal process, by pastors in the theological review process, and by my wife in the "Does this ring true to life?" process. The scripts are born out of my ministry at Perimeter Church, where I've been on part-time staff since 1994 as a sort of "Artist-in-Residence." We do a lot of theater at Perimeter Church. We need lots of scripts. Because of my years of training in theater, I've become the "Designated Writer" there, but I'm also an actor. Since 1982 my full-time job has been as a professional actor, traveling and performing solo theater all over North America. In my travels, I'm in churches with many different styles, including contemporary, traditional, and "seeker-sensitive." And I hear a lot of pleas for scripts. That's why I've finally published some of the things I've written for Perimeter.

You'll notice that there's a wide variety of topics represented here. Most of the scripts can be performed with minimal props and sets, and with few actors. (I know what it's like trying to round up and rehearse too many busy people!) Some of these scripts aim to just "set the table." That is, they will simply introduce a topic, but not attempt to answer too many questions. Some of them, however, attempt to give specific theological answers to real-life questions. Some will work best when combined with sermons or songs. Some work best standing entirely on their own. You'll also notice that I don't shy away from gritty life issues. I'm a firm believer that the grace of God, as evidenced in Jesus, is the ultimate response to this grit.

I hope you are stretched by the performing or even by the reading of these scripts. I hope that in performing them, you'll help open peoples' minds, but, even more importantly (for this is the strong suit of theater), that you'll help open peoples' hearts to the good news of the scandalous love of God for his people. I hope you create some incredible handiwork. You'll probably bang a few thumbs. That's just part of the process and quite to be expected. God bless you as you build!

Curt Cloninger

For more information on Curt Cloninger's solo work, check out his web page at *www.curtcloninger.com*.

Mutts and Pedigrees

Synopsis:
Ron and Dozer and their dogs encounter each other in the vet's waiting room. Dozer offers Ron an unexpected opportunity to get the pedigreed dog he wants, though Ron is less willing to hear the message of mercy Dozer says God offers to "mutts."

Scriptural background:
Luke 15:11-32

Suggested topics:
Grace, not judging by appearances, sharing your faith

Characters:
Ron, a well-dressed, uptight business man
Dozer, a cheerful, gregarious middle-aged biker in black leather

Props:
- two dogs, one that resembles a Pomeranian (small, compact, long-haired dog) and one that looks like a mutt
- several waiting room chairs
- motorcycle helmet
- counter with a sign-in sheet
- magazine
- rope or leash

Setting:
A veterinarian's waiting room

Ron *sits in the waiting room, holding a scruffy-looking mutt in his lap.* Ron *looks up as* Dozer *enters, holding a tiny purebred Pomeranian in his motorcycle helmet.* Dozer *obviously hasn't shaved in a couple of days. He walks up to the counter, signs in, then sits opposite* Ron.

Dozer: Hey! How ya doing? [Ron *doesn't respond,* Dozer *repeats himself*] How ya doing?

Ron: [*surprised he's being talked to by this "biker type," and purposely avoids conversation*] Fine.

Dozer: [*noticing* Ron's *dog*] Nice dog you got there.

Ron: [*curtly*] Yeah.

Dozer: What kind is it?

Ron: I have no idea.

Dozer: Looks like a mutt to me.

Ron: Yeah, well, you may be right.

Dozer: I'm usually a pretty good guesser when it comes to dogs. You had him long?

Ron: No.

Dozer: Where'd you get him?

Ron: Look. I don't know a thing about this dog. My son dragged this—this—mutt home with him last night and wanted to keep him. I told him absolutely not. I told him I'd buy him a nice dog—a purebred—but he insisted that he wanted *this* dog.

Dozer: No kidding? How old is he?

Ron: I have no idea.

Dozer: Your son.

Ron: Oh. Nine. He's nine.

Dozer: So, you gonna keep him?

Ron: My son?

Dozer: The dog.

Ron: Of course not! I'm gonna dump him off here with this vet and tell my son he had worms or something.

Dozer: The vet? [*sees Ron's reaction*] Just kidding.

Ron: [*almost under his breath*] There's no telling where this dog has been.

Dozer: Oh, I can tell you where this dog has been. Out in the world.

Ron: Exactly. That's what I'm worried about. I don't want my son around some rabid, vagabond dog.

Dozer: [*sizing Ron up and deciding that Ron needs to hear this story*] I remember when I was a kid, I was always bringing mutts home. My old man didn't even blink an eye. [Ron *purposely buries his face in a magazine, trying to ignore* Dozer. Dozer *notices the slight, but decides to, very purposely, keep on with his story.*] Yeah—it was funny too. My old man was a real straight shooter. An accountant. But, when it came to dogs—and kids, he was a real softy. You know what my old man always used to say? [Ron *continues to ignore* Dozer] He always used to say, "Never put all your eggs in one basket."

Ron: [*coming out from behind his magazine*] What?

Dozer: [*chuckles*] Just wanted to see if you were listening. [Ron *retreats behind his magazine again*] My old man always used to say, "Kids and mutts are always welcome at this house." Yeah, he didn't seem like the kind of guy who would love mutts, but he did. It's a good thing, too. Otherwise, I'd have been out in the cold more than once. Believe it or not, I used to be a real mutt myself. A hell-raiser.

Ron *still purposely avoids eye contact with* Dozer. Dozer *continues.*

Dozer: Yeah, I did the whole hippie thing. Ripped off my old man when I was sixteen. Lived in a commune in Canada. Followed the "hash trail" in India. And you know what my old man did all that time?

Ron: [*still behind his magazine*] No.

Dozer: Nothing.

Ron: [*almost to himself*] Not surprising.

Dozer: [*hears Ron's aside but chooses to ignore it*] Well, actually, it was more than nothing. I found out later he was worried sick about me. But, eventually, thank God, I came to my senses and came home with my tail tucked between my legs. And guess what my old man did then.

Ron: [*briefly comes out from behind his magazine*] I don't know. Disowned you.

Dozer: Noooo! He paid for college. Seems too good to be true, doesn't it? [*looking down at his Pomeranian and walking over to sit next to Ron*] So, what do you think of my dog?

Ron: I think—I think if somebody walked in here right now, they'd say we got our dogs mixed up.

Dozer: [*laughs*] Yeah. I was thinking that myself. You wanna hear a funny story? One of my clients gave me this dog as a payment.

Ron: A payment?

Dozer: Yeah. This guy owed me a lot of money. He called me up and said he'd pay me off with his prize Pomeranian. Heck, I thought it was an Italian sports car or something. It was this dog. [*laughs*] So, I've brought him in for his tune-up.

Ron: [*curious, but almost afraid to ask*] So, what do you do?

Dozer: You won't believe it. I'm an accountant.

Ron: You?

Dozer: [*chuckles*] Yeah. Amazing, huh? I work with my old man.

Ron: And a client paid you with a dog?

Dozer: Funny thing. This guy, you would've sworn he had all the money in the world. But it turns out this guy was busted flat. Owed me and everybody else a ton of money. But this guy was so proud, he wouldn't even admit he was broke. Well, eventually he sent this dog over to me with a bow on it. He told me it was a "gift." Like this guy [*referring to the Pomeranian*] was gonna square things. [*chuckles*] You know the way I figure it, the lucky folks in this world are the ones who can admit they're in debt.

Ron: Lucky?

Dozer: Yeah. 'Cause they're the only ones who can get forgiven.

Ron: [*still clueless*] Forgiven?

Dozer: Yeah. Forgiven. You never got forgiven before?

Ron: For what?

Dozer: For being in debt!

Ron: I'm not in debt! I've got a perfect credit record. I'm not one of your—clients.

Dozer: [*after a moment's silence*] You know what my old man always says?

Ron: [*sarcastically*] Please. Tell me.

Dozer: [*unfazed*] "When it comes to God and taxes, everybody is in debt, but not everybody knows it."

Ron: [*crossing away from* Dozer] Look, I just came in here to try to get rid of this mutt. Now, thanks very much for the entertaining stories and the pithy aphorisms from your father, but I don't care to talk about God or dogs anymore.

Dozer: [*after another pause*] Hey, did you hear the one about the insomniac dyslexic agnostic? He stayed up all night wondering if there really was a DOG! [*laughs, but gets no response from* Ron; *says this next line to the mutt*] Oh, well, I thought he might like that one. [*there is another silence, then* Dozer *walks over to* Ron] Hey! My name is Jim Dozer. [Dozer *then sticks out his hand to shake* Ron's *hand*] Everybody just calls me Dozer.

Ron: [*hesitantly shakes* Dozer's *hand*] Ron. Ron Carter.

Dozer: Look . . . Ron . . . I'm sorry if I bugged you. I get carried away sometimes when I start talking about important stuff—like God. You know what they say, "He who's forgiven much, loves much."

Ron: Yeah, well, Dozer, I guess I don't know that one.

Dozer: No, I guess you don't, Ron. [*pauses, looks at the two dogs and gets an idea*] Hey, Ron, I've got an idea.

Ron: An idea.

Dozer: Yeah! Why don't we swap dogs?

Ron: [*suddenly interested*] Swap dogs?

Dozer: Yeah! I can give this guy [*referring to* Ron's *mutt*] a great home, and, you know, I think you're probably looking for something else.

Ron: [*now very interested in an idea that he perceives as profitable to him*] I think you might just be onto something, Dozer [*he grabs the Pomeranian and hands* Dozer *the rope attached to the mutt*].

Dozer: [*talking to the mutt, which he now holds in his lap*] Hey, girl. I think I'll call you Honey. That way someone will always come running when my wife calls.

Ron: [*now that he's got a "good" dog, he gets up and starts to leave*] Hey, Dozer, what am I supposed to call this thing?

Dozer: [*smiling*] Mercy, Ron. Mercy.

The Man Behind the Mountain

Synopsis:
Dan has asked Tom to meet him at a coffee shop to discuss the "changes" taking place in the life of Tom's son, Ryan. Tom thinks "this Jesus thing" is just a phase. Dan wants to help him see that there is a world beyond Tom's mall kiosks.

Scriptural background:
Matthew 11:28, 1 Corinthians 1:18

Suggested topics:
The power of Christ to change lives, seeing Christ in the "real world"

Characters:
Dan, a youth minister
Tom, a 3-D art salesman and father of a teenage son
Ann, a cheerful waitress

Props:
• table and two chairs made to look like they're in a coffee shop
• waitress's order tablet
• two coffee cups and a plate with a cinnamon roll

Setting:
A coffee shop on a weekday morning

Dan and Tom are sitting at a table in the coffee shop. Ann is taking their order.

Ann: Okay. Let's see. Dan, you want your usual, am I right? Coffee and a cinnamon roll, nuked.

Dan: Yep.

Ann: [*referring to* Tom] And you, sir? Are you nuked or non-nuked?

Tom: [*bluntly*] Just coffee, please.

Ann: [*chipper*] Be back in a minute.

Dan: I hope this place is okay. As you can probably tell, it's sort of my second home. Ann, the waitress, is a real good friend. Mr. Jackson, I'm glad we could get together like this.

Tom: Please, call me Tom. [*chuckles*] I mean, I'm older than you, but not *that* much older.

Dan: Sure . . . Tom. I'm never sure what to call parents on first meeting, so I usually start out with "mister." Anyway, it's good to finally meet you. I've enjoyed getting to know your wife a little bit at church, and I'm really enjoying having Ryan in the youth group.

Tom: [*uncomfortable*] Yeah, well, he's a good boy. A little rambunctious, just like any kid. But, he's a good boy.

Dan: Yeah, he is. He's really changed a lot in the last few months. I don't know if you've noticed anything.

Tom: He's a high school kid. They go through all kinds of changes, phases, whatever—that sort of thing.

Ann: [*enters carrying two cups of coffee and a cinnamon roll*] There you go fellas. Anything else I can get for you?

Dan: No, we're fine. Thanks, Ann. [*to* Tom] So, Ryan tells me you're in the retail business.

Tom: [*more comfortable with this subject*] I own some franchises. Five states. Have about fifty locations.

Dan: Ryan told me a little about them. What do you call them?

Tom: "Hidden Images." It's 3-D art.

Dan: That's right. Those "picture behind the picture" things.

Tom: Yeah. Those little kiosks in malls. I've got fifty of them. Fifty malls in five states. It's amazing the sales that one of those kiosks can generate. And if you have a bunch of them, well, it really adds up.

Dan: How did you get involved with that? Are you an artist?

Tom: [*laughs*] No, definitely not. I'm a businessman. I saw one of those pictures one time, and I didn't just see the picture, or the picture behind the picture. I saw a good business opportunity. So, I linked up with the people who print the things and bought them out.

Dan: You know, I've gotta tell you. I don't get those pictures.

Tom: What do you mean?

Dan: I don't get 'em. I don't ever see what you're supposed to see in 'em. You know, the picture behind the picture. I've got this friend, he loves the things. I bet he's bought ten of them. One day I stood with him in our mall here. I guess that's your place, right?

Tom: Yeah, that's one of mine.

Dan: I stood there staring at this mountain landscape kind of picture. And he kept saying to me, "Don't you see it?" "I see a mountain," I'd say. "No! Look behind the mountain. What do you see?" "I see a mountain." He was getting madder and madder. "LOOK BEYOND THE MOUNTAIN! BEHIND THE MOUNTAIN! Don't you see a man?!!" "I see a mountain." [*laughs*] He was furious with me. He could NOT believe that I couldn't see "The man behind the mountain." But I couldn't see it. I just couldn't. [*laughs*] I guess I'm "3-D challenged," or something. My friend told me I was trying too hard. You know what he did? He bought me that picture as a Christmas present. I hung it up in my office at church. Seems like every kid who comes in my office looks at it and says, "Cool picture. And that man—he's amazing." [*laughs, shaking his head*] I don't even look at it anymore.

Tom: [*he's heard all this before*] I could get you to see it in three minutes. I could make you see whatever it is, "the man behind the mountain." It's all in how you focus.

Dan: [*laughs*] I don't know. I'm a pretty tough customer.

Tom: I'm a pretty good salesman.

Dan: Yeah, well, anyway, I just thought you'd like to know, I've got some of your stuff.

Tom: Good. Gotta pay the rent. Every little bit helps.

Dan: [*deciding that it's time to get to the heart of the matter*] I promised Ryan, a couple of weeks ago, that I'd call and try to get together with you. So, I really appreciate you taking the time to do that.

Tom: No problem. [*looks at his watch*] But, listen, I've got a 10:30 appointment. So, is there some kind of problem with Ryan that we need to talk about?

Dan: No! No, not at all. He's doing great. Ryan is, well, he's had some life-changing stuff happen in the last couple of weeks. [*sensing that he's getting ahead of himself*] Has he talked to you in the last couple of weeks, since he got back from that retreat we went on?

Tom: [*getting a bit testy*] Yeah, he's talked to me. We talk, Ryan and I. I'm not an absentee dad, if that's what you mean.

Dan: No! No, I didn't mean that. I just meant—well, have you talked about, about spiritual things?

Tom: [*now realizing what's going on*] Oh, okay. Now I get it. Yeah. Last week he, uh, he came into my study one night. He sat down across from my desk and told me that he'd, uh—how did he put it? "Accepted the Lord," or he'd "Seen Jesus" or some such nonsense.

Dan: [*gently digging deeper*] What do you think he meant by that? "Seen Jesus"?

Tom: Look, Dan. I'm glad my wife is in your church, and I'm glad my son is involved in your youth group. Hopefully, it keeps him off the street and away from sex and drugs and rock and roll. But, if you're training him to be some sort of "Junior Billy Graham" so he can "convert the old man," you can forget it. I'm not interested. My wife's already tried. I'm not interested.

Dan: Do you think Ryan saw Jesus?

Tom: I think Ryan is a sixteen-year-old kid. When he was seven he was into Ninja Turtles. When he was eleven he was into Power Rangers. Now he's sixteen, and I guess it's Jesus' turn. He's a kid, Dan. He goes through phases.

Dan: What phase do you think your wife is in?

Tom: [*pauses and calms down a bit*] Look—Dan. I don't mean to be—disrespectful. [*thinks of a way to get this across*] You know, I, uh, I love to read *The New Yorker* magazine.

Dan: Yeah. Me, too. Great cartoons.

Tom: Well, I keep a bunch of back issues in the bathroom. I like to read 'em in there. It's private. It's quiet. For the last six months my wife, Peggy, and my son, Ryan, have been taking my *New Yorkers* out of the bathroom and replacing them with little—Bible things—Scriptures and pamphlets and stuff. And to be fair, I've read some of that stuff. I've read it. I just don't get it. And to be perfectly frank, I'd like my *New Yorker* back.

Dan: As long as we're being perfectly frank, me and your wife—and your son, Mr. Jackson, and your son—*know* Jesus. And your son's life is changed. It really is. And it's not a phase. Ryan's never gonna be the same again. He really does know Jesus. No bull.

Tom: [*silent for a moment, then gets up to leave*] Look, Dan. Truce. Okay? Truce. I've spent the last twenty years building businesses. And that has been a hard mountain to climb. But, right now, I'm doing well. I've got a good family and a very successful business. I'm as busy as I want to be. I don't need anything else on my plate. All this "religious stuff," I just don't get it. It's just something else on my plate. So, thanks for your time. Sorry I wasn't a willing convert, but I've got enough mountains to climb right now [*starts to leave*].

Dan: Hey, Tom. Maybe there's a man behind the mountain.

Tom: [*stops and turns and says, almost to himself, and a bit sadly*] Maybe.

All This Noise

Synopsis:
A very tired-looking man occupies center stage. He serves as his own narrator and performs his actions as he narrates them. He is a successful man, but worn down and confused, searching for answers in his noisy world.

Scriptural background:
Jeremiah 29:11

Suggested topics:
Hearing God's voice in a very busy world, knowing God has a plan for you

Characters:
Man
God-Voice
Son
Wife
Boss

Props:
• ladder
• suit coat, briefcase
• lawn chair
• piece of paper
• *Wall Street Journal*
• recording of Skip Carey's voice (or another sports announcer)

Setting:
Man's backyard and inside his head

Man *walks slowly out to center stage. His tie is loosened. He slings his suit coat over his shoulder with one hand and in the other hand carries his briefcase.*

Man: There once was a man who lived in the suburbs. He had a nice wife, two nice kids, and one nice dog. He had two nice cars, a nice house, and a backyard full of nicely tended Bermuda. He made a nice salary working for a company where he had survived three rounds of layoffs. Every Friday night he took his wife to a nice restaurant and a movie. Every other night he tended his lawn, played with his kids, or watched the Braves on his large screen TV with surround sound. His life was . . . nice.

But one day the man came home from work, walked into his backyard, and looked out over his expanse of Bermuda. He slowly sat on a lawn chair and realized that he was very, very tired. And as he sat there he wondered if there was more to life than simply "nice." He thought of a fellow from work who was religious, who claimed to "hear from God." The man wondered about that: "hearing from God." It sounded a little scary to him. All he knew was that people who hear from God usually wear funny clothes or wind up as missionaries in Africa. He didn't want to go to Africa. He wasn't sure he could get cable there. Cable! Ahhh! The man remembered, there was a Braves game on.

As the man rose from his lawn chair and reached in his pocket for his house keys, he felt a piece of paper wadded up there. He wondered for a moment what it was, but then remembered that his religious co-worker had handed it to him that day after a meeting. In the business of the day, he had forgotten that the note was in his pocket. He unfolded the paper and read this: "You've been looking pretty worn out lately. I thought you might be encouraged by these words from the Bible."

At this point, the Scripture is narrated by the God-Voice. *The* God-Voice *is provided by an actor who sits atop a six-foot stepladder, upstage of the* Man. *If possible, the* God-Voice *has been sitting there the whole time and the lights come up to reveal him. He begins to recite the verse very conversationally, not in a booming or stentorian way.*

God-Voice: For I know the plans I have for you. Plans to prosper you and not to do you harm. Plans to give you hope and a future.

Man: The man's thoughts shifted from baseball to God. And as he looked at the paper, he thought, "This is a good thing." At that moment he almost began to believe that he might actually be able to hear God as well as he could hear Skip Carey.

During the next section and throughout the rest of the piece, the God-Voice *is constantly, steadily, but not loudly, repeating the Jeremiah passage. There is a short pause before the* God-Voice *begins to repeat the passage. The* Man *"inclines his ear" toward the ladder, as if straining to hear. Once the* God-Voice *begins again, it continues throughout the rest of the piece.*

God-Voice: For I know the plans I have for you—

The God-Voice *continues a bit louder for a moment, then begins to be overshadowed by the* Son's *voice. Then the* Son's *voice and* God-Voice *begin to be overshadowed by the* Wife's *voice. Then the* Son's *voice, the* Wife's *voice, and* God-Voice *begin to be overshadowed by the* Boss's *voice. After the* Son's *first time through his line, the other two voices—Wife, Boss—get louder and louder, competing for the* Man's *ear. Eventually the* God-Voice *is all but drowned out. The man never sees the other people. It is as if they are simply voices in his head.*

Son: [*Enters downstage left of the* Man, *talking full speed as he enters and never stopping. He winds up directly downstage from* Man.] Hey Dad! What I was thinking was you and me could get up early Saturday morning and ride bikes for awhile in the park, then we could go to Malibu Grand Prix and do the go-carts and then we could play a little putt-putt, and I got my homework done. I need forty bucks for my new soccer uniform, and I really need some new Nikes.

Wife: [*Light comes up on her stage right. She speaks over the* Son *and the* God-Voice *and repeats her lines over and over, just as the* Son *and the* God-Voice *do.*] Don't even ask me about my day. The transmission went on the Camry. I discovered fleas in the basement. Jen's gerbil is loose somewhere. I accepted a dinner invitation to the Smith's for Thursday night. I was thinking it would be fun to get away next weekend, just the two of us; maybe up to Asheville or somewhere, 'cause it really seems like we need to. By the way, do you know where the remote is?

Boss: [*Light comes up on him stage left. He has a newspaper and reads a clip from the* Wall Street Journal. *He repeats his lines over and over, competing for the* Man's *ears.*] This is from this morning's *Journal*, people. "Stock prices fell after a new round of economic numbers renewed fears that the Federal Reserve will raise interest rates."

This doesn't look good for us. I'm afraid we're going to have to start another round of layoffs.

The voices all repeat themselves over and over for a bit, all of them, except the God-Voice, *getting louder and louder. After a cacophony is reached, the* Man *stands up. As soon as he stands up, the* Boss, *the* Wife, *and the* Son *all immediately grow silent, and exit quickly. Only the* God-Voice *continues, from the ladder, softly and persistently. There is a brief moment when the* God-Voice *is heard by the audience, but then it begins to be VERY slowly overshadowed by a recording of* Skip Carey *calling an Atlanta Braves game.*

Man: [*He slowly folds up the piece of paper and puts it in his pocket. Then he slowly picks up his briefcase and his coat and slowly walks out through the audience as he speaks.*] But as the man rose from his lawn chair, he realized that it was ludicrous to think he might actually hear the voice of God.

As the man walks slowly out through the audience, the Skip Carey *voice grows louder and louder, again overshadowing the* God-Voice, *as the light slowly fades on the ladder.*

In the Family

Synopsis:
Jan and Ed meet for breakfast and reminisce about their childhood. Jan reminds Ed that their parents always loved them, despite the fact Ed set the backyard on fire and tied Mary Lou Hanna to a tree.

Scriptural background:
Romans 8:1-4

Suggested topics:
Unconditional love and forgiveness, Mother's Day

Characters:
Ed, a single guy in his late twenties or early thirties
Jan, his sister, married with kids

Props:
Table and two chairs

Setting:
Waffle House

Ed *is seated at a table as* Jan *hurriedly walks up.*

Jan: I'm sorry I am late. Car pool.

Ed: No problem. I ordered for you. French Toast. Sausage. Coffee. Did I get it right?

Jan: Bingo.

Ed: And you thought I never paid any attention to you. See, I even remembered what you used to order at the Waffle House.

Jan: [*quizzing him*] So, what was my doll's name growing up?

Ed: [*without hesitation*] "Pearl." Always "Pearl." It didn't matter if it was a baby or a Barbie. "Pearl."

Jan: [*still quizzing*] Okay, so what was my first boyfriend's name?

Ed: Pearl. Just kidding. Ryan. If I remember correctly, he had braces and very bad breath. And he didn't last long. Didn't measure up with Dad.

Jan: To put it mildly. So, how ya doing? Is work okay?

Ed: It's work.

Jan: You still dating that same gal? What was her name?

Ed: Laurie. Nope. That one didn't get too far. How about you? You doing okay?

Jan: Yeah, I guess so. The kids drive me crazy sometimes.

Ed: How so?

Jan: Oh, just normal stuff. You know, pushing the boundaries.

Ed: Like what?

Jan: Like . . . like, I caught Rachel out in the backyard the other day smoking a cigarette.

Ed: No kidding? What'd you do to her?

Jan: The same thing Mom did to you when she caught you smoking a cigarette in the backyard. I bought a pack of Camels and made her smoke the whole thing in one sitting. That cured her.

Ed: [*laughs*] Yeah, I guess so. It worked for me. Boy, Jan, I don't know how you do it. If I was married and had kids I'd probably disown 'em the first time they messed up.

Jan: No, you wouldn't.

Ed: Yes, I would. I mean, my patience with kids is about that deep [*indicates an inch gap with his fingers*]. I'd disown 'em.

Jan: No, you wouldn't, Ed.

Ed: Oh, yeah. Why not?

Jan: 'Cause they're your kids. You're not gonna disown your own kids. Look, do you remember what you were like when you were a kid?

Ed: Yeah. I was an angel.

Jan: You seem to be having a case of severely repressed memory. You were always in trouble.

Ed: Yeah, well, maybe a little.

Jan: Always. The time Mom caught you with the cigarettes. The time you flooded the basement. The time you and Ed McGuire tied up Mary Lou Hanna to the pine tree and left her there all afternoon. You were always in trouble. But, hey, you didn't pass some kind of entrance exam to *get* into the family, and you sure didn't pass one to *stay* in. You were just in. Why do you think that was?

Ed: Because I was so cute?

Jan: Yeah, right. You remember that time you set the backyard on fire?

Ed: Yeah, I was experimenting with some matches.

Jan: Some experiment. You remember what happened?

Ed: I remember that Dad was out of town on business, so the spanking I got was milder than it would've been. That's about all I remember.

Jan: Well, I remember a lot more than that. I remember thinking, "Wow, this is it. This is finally it. Ed is now going to get sent to live with Aunt Karen. He's a goner." But this was so weird. I remember that after Mom spanked you, you were sitting there on the couch with her. And she hugged you and told you she loved you. And then she asked you why you thought she loved you. You told her, "Because I didn't set the house on fire too?" She laughed and she said, "Nope. I love you because you're my kid." Then she said to you, "Now, go on up to your room." After you left the room, I sidled over to Mom. Nestled right up to her on the couch.

Ed: Talk about a little brownnoser.

Jan: [*ignoring him*] I said to her, "Mamma, why do you love me?" I just knew she was gonna say, "Because you're a good girl. You didn't play with matches like your bad brother, Ed." But she said, "I love you because you're my kid. Now go on out and play."

Ed: It's amazing how much you remember!

Jan: It's amazing how much you forget. Anyway, that whole little episode really stuck with me. I mean, I couldn't have vocalized it at the time, but now, as a mom myself, I think I get it. I was in, you were in, not because of what we did, but because of who Mom and Dad were. It's like knowing that almost made me want to do right.

Ed: [*thinking*] Yeah, well, I guess it took awhile to have the same effect on me. Anyway, enough of these childhood memories, doctor. What are we gonna do for Mom for Mother's Day?

Jan: Well, we could always buy her a pack of Camels and a box of matches.

Ed: Very funny.

Jan: You know what I think we oughta do? I think we oughta gather everybody together and just show up on her doorstep. Just show up.

Ed: You think that'd be good?

Jan: It would be good. Trust me. It's a daughter thing.

Don't Feed the Rat

Synopsis:
Nancy and Marci encounter each other as they are leaving work. Nancy asks Marci what's been wrong lately and discovers that Marci is holding on to a part of her past that's weighing her down.

Scriptural background:
Romans 6

Suggested topics:
Being free of your sinful nature, putting old ways and bad habits behind you, releasing the past

Characters:
Marci, a young executive who seems stressed out and distracted
Nancy, her co-worker and friend

Props:
Two briefcases

Setting:
An office hallway

Nancy *and* Marci *meet at the office door as they are leaving work.*

Nancy: Hey, Marci, how'd your day go? You making any progress on that DayStar proposal?

Marci: Yeah, sorta. The thing's a black hole. I just can't seem to get ahead on it. Thanks for asking, though.

Nancy: Sure, no problem. [*concerned but not pushy*] It seems like you've been kinda distracted lately.

Marci: Distracted? [*a bit hesitant to reveal anything*] Oh, I don't know.

Nancy: Has Jackson loaded you up with more accounts since the layoffs?

Marci: Oh, no more than anybody else. It's just—

Nancy: [*interrupting*] You need me to put in a good word for you with Jackson?

Marci: No—no, I'm fine, really. Work's actually going pretty well.

Nancy: [*fishing for the real problem*] So, how's your love life?

Marci: [*chuckles*] Distracting.

Nancy: You still going with that guy?

Marci: Jeff?

Nancy: Yeah, Jeff—the salesman, right?

Marci: Yeah, the salesman.

Nancy: So, are you still dating him?

Marci: No. I'm definitely NOT still dating him.

Nancy: Is that good news?

Marci: Yeah, that's definitely good news.

Nancy: You dating somebody else?

Marci: Nope.

Nancy: [*trying to understand the problem*] But you're kinda a little "iffy" about breaking up with Jeff?

Marci: No! Not at all. Breaking up with Jeff is the best thing I ever did. The guy was a total jerk. All he did was drag me down. I mean, this guy was totally self-absorbed. Totally selfish. The whole time I dated him we only did stuff that he wanted to do. And all of it was lousy stuff. I mean, lousy stuff. The guy thought the whole world revolved around him. I've never known a more self-centered, insensitive turkey!

Nancy: Then why in the world did you date him?

Marci: I have no idea. I must've been out of my mind. The guy was a total rodent.

Nancy: Wait a minute! Is this the same Jeff who gave you the white rat for a birthday present?

Marci: The very Jeff.

Nancy: What kind of idiot would give a grown woman a rat for a birthday present?

Marci: Jeff. He likes rats. It didn't really matter to him that I hate rats. He thought it would be fun to give me a rat. And on top of that, he expected me to take care of it! A rat! A disgusting rat!

Nancy: Honey! You don't need to be distracted! What you need to do is celebrate. I am gonna take you out to dinner tonight! We are gonna celebrate "Freedom From Jeff Day." When did you break up with him?

Marci: Two months ago.

Nancy: All right! We're gonna celebrate "Freedom From Jeff for Two Months." You need a party is what you need. You are a free woman! You need to live like it! No more rats in your future! Now, you name the restaurant. I'm buying! Any place in town. This calls for a celebration!

Marci: [*hesitant*] Uh, I can't tonight.

Nancy: What, you've already got plans?

Marci: Yeah, sorta.

Nancy: What, do you have a date?

Marci: No, not exactly.

Nancy: A meeting?

Marci: No, not exactly.

Nancy: So, what've you got that you'd turn down a free dinner, great company, and a stupendous celebration of a very timely breakup?

Marci: I've—I've gotta get home.

Nancy: What in the world for?

Marci: I've gotta do something.

Nancy: [*forcing the answer out of her*] What?!

Marci: I've gotta feed the rat.

Nancy: Wait a minute. You've gotta feed—

Marci: —the rat.

Nancy: You kept the rat?!!!!

Marci: Yeah.

Nancy: [*incredulous*] Let me get this straight. You broke up with the guy? [Marci *nods yes*] But you kept his rat? [Marci *nods yes*] You dumped this turkey? [Marci *nods yes*] But you didn't kill the rat? [Marci *nods yes*] You're no longer with this idiot. [Marci *nods yes*] But you choose to be some sort of slave to this rat he gave you? [Marci *nods yes*]. [*pause*] Honey, no wonder you're distracted.

The Allowance

Synopsis:
John and Mary leaf through their mail over coffee. John is upset that their son didn't buy him a birthday card because their son is saving up for a Game Boy. Then they read the letter from church, requesting a missions donation.

Scriptural background:
2 Corinthians 9:6

Suggested Topics:
Returning to God what he has given to us, generosity, priorities

Characters:
John, a good-natured but irritable man
Mary, his wife, who is feisty and a bit sarcastic, but not unkind

Props:
- various pieces of mail
- two cups of coffee
- table
- two chairs

Setting:
John and Mary's kitchen

John: [*entering and sitting at the table where* Mary *is already seated*] Got anything interesting there?

Mary: [*sorting through the mail*] Utility bill, phone bill, car phone bill, junk mail, time-share condo brochure, car insurance bill, junk mail, boat insurance bill, something from church, club dues, a postcard from my brother from Fargo, North Dakota. [*reading the postcard out loud*] "In Fargo on business. Quite a town! Wish you were here. Harry." No thanks, Harry. [*sarcastic*] Quite an exciting life he leads. And last but not least, your birthday card from your sister Debbie. As usual, a week late.

John: [*laughing*] I don't think she knows it's late. I just think Debbie is firmly convinced that I was born a week too early. Hey, at least she sent me a card. That's more than most folks did.

Mary: What do you mean by that? I not only got you a card, I baked you a cake and bought you a dozen golf balls. And I would've thrown you a surprise party, but I know how much you hate those things.

John: And I thank you for that. The best present I ever get is not having to act surprised. No, I don't mean you. I mean that knuckleheaded son of ours.

Mary: [*laughs*] Oh, don't be so hard on him. He's just a kid.

John: A twelve-year-old kid!

Mary: So he's twelve. Does that make it a crime that he forgot your birthday?

John: Forgot my birthday?! That's just the point! He didn't forget my birthday! He knew full well that it was my birthday! That's what burns me!

Mary: [*a bit dumbfounded*] Oh.

John: [*almost laughing, not too "heavy"*] The day after my birthday I was driving him to school and he says to me, "Sorry I didn't get you a present, Dad. I just couldn't spare the money." So I say to him, "You couldn't even spare the money for a card?" And get this! He says, "No, Dad, you know I'm saving for a Game Boy." Can you believe that?! I give the kid ten dollars a week allowance. TEN

DOLLARS A WEEK! And he can't spend a buck fifty for a birthday card for me! I'm the one who gives him the money in the first place! That's what really burns me! You'd think he'd get me a card just because he's grateful to get a ten buck allowance! Or, at least you'd think he'd get me a card just to grease the wheels—to keep the money pump primed!

Mary: [*as she continues to open mail, egging him on*] So, what are you gonna do?

John: [*excited and a bit irrational*] I'll tell you what I'm gonna do! I'm gonna—I'm gonna—I don't know what I'm gonna do!

Mary: Are you gonna cut off his allowance?

John: Yeah, that's what I'm gonna do. I'm gonna cut off his allowance! I'm gonna cut off every stinking dime of his allowance! Nah, that would be kinda cheesy. He doesn't thank me so I wipe him out. That's no good. It's gotta be something that'll hit him between the eyes, make him realize where all that allowance money is coming from in the first place.

Mary: [*still a bit sarcastic*] Hey, why don't you write him a letter—you know, sit down and think it out and then explain it all to him clearly, in twelve-year-old language, in a letter.

John: Yeah, that may do it. I'll have to think about that—a letter. Hmmm, that may work. [*noticing that* Mary's *opening one more envelope*] Anything else for me?

Mary: Just this from the church. Some letter from [*insert your minister's name*] about some special offering for missions.

John: [*ticked off*] Missions?! Oh, great. We've been at this church for six months, and I've been wondering when it would happen. And here it is, the big push for money. It seems like every time I turn around, God's got his hand out. Well, this time it's out of the question. I just can't spare any extra money right now!

Mary: What about dipping into your, uh, what do you call it? your "Special Needs Account"?

John: Are you crazy?! You know I'm saving that money for a Mazda Miata.

Mary: [*dry and dumbfounded*] Oh.

My Side of the Story

Synopsis:
Husband and Wife address the audience, airing their grievances about each other, each unaware that the other is present. The audience soon begins to see that there *are* two sides to every story.

Scriptural background:
1 Peter 3:1, 2, 7

Suggested Topics:
Marriage, miscommunication, empathy

Characters:
Husband, a businessman with a wife and several children
Wife, a homemaker and loving but frazzled mother

Props:
None

Setting:
Wherever people might share about themselves

Husband and Wife *are together on stage, facing the audience.* Husband *begins. Words in parentheses are said in unison.*

Husband: Okay. This is what happened. No doubt she'll tell you different.

Wife: He'll tell you different. But then again, he's always a little skewed on (how)

Husband: (How) she sees these things. But first, let me tell you that I really do love my wife. It's just that (she)

Wife: (He) drives me crazy sometimes, even though I really do love him.

Husband: I'd had a really bad day at work. The fax was down, the copier was down, and my secretary was—down. Probably sixty phone calls, and at least twenty of them dealing with problems that only I could solve. In short, I spent my day putting out—

Wife: Fires. Literally. One of the kids got hold of some matches that *he* had left out by the grill. The kids thought it would be fun to start a campfire in the backyard. That was the first fire of the day, and it got worse from there. Three cuts, one bloody nose, an overflowed dishwasher, and probably twenty phone calls from people with problems that only I could solve. In short, I'd had a really bad day. Oh! and to top that off, the stove fritzed out, the kids were grouchy, starving, and by the time I got them some peanut butter and jelly sandwiches made, it was at least seven—

Husband: By the time I dragged out of the office, it was at least seven (o'clock).

Wife: (O'clock) and even though I managed to feed them, I hadn't even started to get them in the bathtub.

Husband: I hadn't eaten all day, because I just never had time to—

Wife: Get around to it. So, needless to say, I was starving.

Husband: All I wanted was to get home and crash. I wasn't expecting miracles. Just a little peace and—

Wife: Quiet. That's all I wanted. Just a few minutes of peace. And maybe a big bowl of Häagen-Dazs. Somehow or other, when I've had a bad day, ice cream seems to help. But anyway—

Husband: That's all I wanted. Peace and quiet. Maybe put my feet up, have a big glass of iced tea, some leftovers, turn on the tube and watch the Braves unravel on TBS. That always seems to help.

Wife: He walks in the door at 7:48 and—

Husband: I got home sometime after seven, trudged through the back door and—

Wife and Husband: WHAT DID I SEE?

Husband: I saw a disaster area. Worse than my office. Kids running around screaming. Dishes, toys everywhere. Bucket and mop in the middle of the kitchen floor. And no one paid one ounce of attention to the fact that I had walked through the door. I didn't say a word because I was afraid of what I'd say. Instead, I held my tongue and walked slowly over to the television.

Wife: I'll tell you what I saw. As I chased down one of the kids and wrestled her toward the bathtub, I saw him walk over to the television, turn it on and plop himself down. Without a word!

Husband: I turned it on and counted to about two hundred. I didn't think counting to ten would be quite enough.

Wife: Can you believe it?! Not a word. No, "Whoa, it looks like you've had a rough day." No, "Hey, can I corral that kid for you?!" Not a word!

Husband: I wasn't expecting "Home Beautiful." Just a little order. That's all. I held my tongue until I could be supportive.

Wife: I wasn't expecting a dozen roses. Just a little help. That's all. I didn't say anything because I was afraid of what I might say.

Husband: I didn't expect—

Wife: A miracle.

Wife and Husband: Just a little concern.

Husband: Maybe a phone call during the day.

Wife: Maybe a phone call during the day.

Husband: You know, "Hey, how's your day going? Oh! I'm sorry to hear that. Maybe I'll have you a pizza ordered and some sun tea made and you can sit with the kids and watch the Braves on television." You know, something like that. Nothing major.

Wife: You know, "Hey, how's your day going? Oh! I'm sorry to hear that. Maybe I'll stop by the store on the way home and get you a pint of Häagen-Dazs." Something like that. Nothing major.

Husband: But it would have made all the difference in the world.

Wife: But it would have made all the difference in the world.

Husband: If she'd done that.

Wife: If he'd done that.

Husband: I would have scrubbed the floors for her when I got home.

Wife: I would have given him a back rub when he got home.

Husband: Hey, I would've brought her a gallon of Häagen-Dazs.

Wife: Hey, I would've ordered him a gourmet pizza.

Husband: But, as it was—

Wife: But, as it was—

Husband: We weren't even—

Wife: Talking.

Wife and Husband: I just couldn't believe how selfish he/she was!

Husband: About eleven o'clock, by the time I had calmed down—

Wife: By the time I had calmed down, around midnight—

Husband: I brought up the fact that I was a little hurt by the lack of attention I got when I walked through my own back door.

Wife: I brought up the fact that I was a little hurt that he had completely ignored me when he walked through the back door.

Husband: And do you know what she said?

Wife: Do you know what he said?

Wife and Husband: That it was all my fault!

Husband: Can you believe it?

Wife: Can you believe it?

Husband: She never admits—

Wife: He never admits—

Husband: She's wrong.

Wife: He's wrong.

Husband: Well, I guess there's two—

Wife: Sides to every story.

Wife and Husband: Just not this one!

Trouble Near the K-Mart

Synopsis:
Two women, Jane Troxler and Carol Anders, meet in a restaurant. They are friends meeting for lunch. Carol is a Realtor who sold Jane a house. As the scene opens, Carol is seated at a table and Jane enters. Jane is "quietly seething" at Carol, and as the scene unfolds we understand why.

Scriptural background:
Colossians 3:13

Suggested topics:
Forgiveness (or lack thereof), trust, friendship

Characters:
Jane Troxler, a lawyer who bought a house from Carol
Carol Anders, a real estate agent and Jane's best friend

Props:
• table
• two chairs

Setting:
A restaurant

Jane *enters the restaurant, sees* Carol, *and joins her at the table.* Jane *is obviously irritated, but calm.*

Carol: [*as* Jane *sits down*] Hey! I was beginning to think I'd gotten the wrong restaurant! It's great to see you!

Jane: [*obviously cold and stiff, but still "formally polite"*] Yes. I'm sorry I'm late. I got caught in the construction traffic.

Carol: Hey, no problem. The traffic is awful today, isn't it? So, how in the world have you been? I haven't seen you in weeks.

Jane: I've been fine, thanks.

Carol: I guess you've been busy, huh? I've called you probably ten times, but I figured you were so busy decorating the house that you haven't had time to call me back.

Jane: [*cold*] Yes. Fairly busy.

Carol: [*genuinely excited*] So how is it? Do you love it?! I mean, I knew when I saw that house that it was the one for you! I am so glad you let me sell you that house! It is like a dream come true: I sell the perfect house to my best friend! I mean, it is perfect for you! As soon as I listed it, I knew it was your house.

Jane: Yeah.

Carol: So, what have you done to it? Have you painted anything yet? What about those bushes in the front yard—did you pull those out yet?

Jane: No, no, I haven't done a whole lot.

Carol: [*somewhat taken aback*] Oh. Well, what have you been doing?

Jane: [*still seething*] Not a whole lot. I haven't been getting out much.

Carol: [*concerned*] Have you been sick?

Jane: No, no. It's just a little hard to get out because of the construction.

Carol: [*innocently*] Construction? What construction?

Jane: What do you mean, "What construction?" The construction in back of my house!

Carol: What do you mean? There are woods in back of your house.

Jane: Wrong! There *were* woods in back of my house. Now there's a K-Mart!

Carol: No!

Jane: Oh, yeah. And don't act so innocent! You knew you were selling me the parking lot of a K-Mart! That's why I got the house so cheap!

Carol: Jane, I didn't know. I had no idea! I haven't even been by your neighborhood in two months. Remember? I told you at the closing—I told you I was gonna be out of town for awhile. I haven't seen any K-Mart!

Jane: [*getting more and more angry*] Well, drive on by! It's easy to spot. You can see the dust cloud from my backyard and hear the bulldozers from my kitchen! Pretty soon I'll be able to hear them announcing the blue-light special!

Carol: [*in shock*] I had no idea they were gonna put a K-Mart back there.

Jane: Yeah, right! You Realtors know everything. You're like vultures waiting for something to die.

Carol: Wait a minute! I DIDN'T KNOW ABOUT THE K-MART! And besides, you're one to talk about vultures. YOU! A LAWYER! You know what they call ten lawyers at the bottom of the ocean? A good start!

Jane: I will ignore that last tasteless joke, considering it's source and also because I am so even-tempered.

Carol: Even-tempered, my eye! You've probably been stewing for two months, trying to figure out how to sue me or something! Go ahead and sue me and see what good it does you!

Jane: [*suddenly calm*] I am not going to sue you. I thought about that and decided that would not be the right thing to do.

Carol: Well, isn't that big of you!

Jane: I also thought about calling the Realtor Association and filing a complaint on you.

Carol: You wouldn't!

Jane: No. I wouldn't. I decided that would not be the right thing to do.

Carol: Well, aren't you "Little Miss Perfect!"

Jane: [*suddenly very sanctimonious*] I even prayed about what I should do concerning your lying about the K-Mart—

Carol: I DID NOT LIE ABOUT THE K-MART!

Jane: [*continuing*] I prayed about what I should do. I asked God if I should forgive you.

Carol: And what did God tell you?

Jane: God said I should forgive you—

Carol: Well, good.

Jane: God said I should forgive you, but I thought about it and I decided NAAH! This K-Mart thing is simply too big to forgive. A person who would lie about a K-Mart in your backyard is a dangerous person.

Carol: Jane! For the last time, I DIDN'T KNOW ABOUT THE K-MART!

An awkward pause during which Carol *gives up; she looks over to* Jane *for a reaction.*

Carol: Look, I understand you being angry. But, I'm telling you, this is all news to me.

Jane: I'm not angry. When I first saw the bulldozers I was angry, but I counted to ten . . . thousand, and now I'm not angry. I've risen above that.

Carol: [*relieved*] Good. So, what are we gonna do? You want me to list your house again? I'll do it for no commission.

Jane: [*very calm*] No. I've thought about this very rationally and calmly, and I've come to a decision. That's why I've called this meeting this morning. While we sit here, having our coffee, the movers have finished loading my furniture into the van. [*looks at her watch*] They are now unloading it into your living room. I am moving in with you, MY BEST FRIEND.

About the Author

Curt Cloninger has loved theater for about as long as he has loved Jesus. Curt started acting in high school and hasn't quit yet. He received a B.A. in theater and communication from Abilene Christian University in 1976. He received further acting training at the Pacific Conservatory of the Performing Arts. Since 1982, Curt's full-time job has been as a solo performer. He has written many award-winning monologue theater pieces which he performs for conferences, churches, and colleges all over North America. He has performed in practically every denominational setting, and for audiences varying in size from 30 to 30,000.

Since 1994 Curt has served as an Artist-in-Residence with Perimeter Church, a large seeker-sensitive church in suburban Atlanta, Georgia. When Curt is not on the road performing his solo work, he is writing, directing, and performing in many of the theater pieces which Perimeter Church presents.

Curt has produced several award-winning videos that have been used by thousands of people for curriculum and discussion starters. His current videos include "God-Views," "Witnesses," and "Red-Letter Edition."

Curt and his wife, Tish, have two children, Kap and Lily, and an assortment of critters (dogs, cats, fish and mice).

For more information on Curt Cloninger's solo work, or his videos, you may contact him at the address below:
P.O. Box 2353
Duluth, Georgia 30096
or
www.curtcloninger.com